Here for the Heart

Adrian Cunningham

Presentation by *BookLeaf Publishing*

Web: www.bookleafpub.com

E-mail: info@bookleafpub.com

ISBN: 9789357690423

First edition 2022

DEDICATION

To my beautiful niece Aerah, so glad you were able to come home from the NICU after 3.5 months on Halloween 2022. To my amazing cousin Carla, it is such painful irony that the day Aerah comes home is also the day you leave us for your heavenly home, due to cancer. You are both my love and inspiration. You both have my heart.

ACKNOWLEDGEMENT

Thanks again to Rachel for proofreading my poetry - like I told you, I just write things, but you, you read things, you really read things, and I am forever thankful.

PREFACE

"One of the hardest things in life is having words in your heart that you can't utter." - James Earl Jones. Here are these words, uttered in the best way they can be. Please do enjoy.

Heart, break

It had been a while since
I felt this way, since I felt
I didn't need to always be
Alone

He came to me
Unconventionally
His voice and fingers
Musically

Texting, replying
Reading, meeting
"Can I have a goodbye kiss?"
Absolutely

He'd cheated before just
Not recently
Would he cheat again?
Uncertain

He wasn't ready for
The plunge, the commit
From replying it became, just read
Read 1:34 pm

Unfollow, unresponsive
Nonexistent
Still friends though?
Questionable

Tears racing, eyes full
Eating? Nah. Sleeping? Yah.
</3, sliced, cleaved
Irreparable

The days move slowly
But it gets better, right?
It gets better, it gets better, it....
Repetir

Repetir until it is true
Repetir until you can watch the show you both
loved
Repetir until....until you find something better
Repetir until there is no longer heart
Break

Heartless

They milk me of my power
Taking what is mine
And claiming it as theirs
So heartless they are

I bear the wounds of their cruelty
Their words like daggers
Slicing my self esteem
Any part vulnerable is damaged

I call my steed to my side
To give me more power to face them
It comes only for a brief moment
Because it knows I can face them alone

No steed, no power, visible wounds
But one thing I have that they don't: spirit
They must shudder at the sight of that word:
spirit
It contradicts everything they know: spirit
It weakens them
Spirit
Painful wounds, open wounds, sliced wounds
Spirited wounds
They milk me of my power
No more

Heartful

Heartbroken
Thirsting for love
Figuring yourself out
Doubt, despair
Loneliness, beware

Heartless
Not good enough
Never wanted this
Leave, escape
Before you break

Hearty
Can do this?
Sure let's try again
Talking, meeting
Date date date

Heartful
Fun times!
But definitely just friends
Enjoying, doing
Heart full again

Homecoming

5

A heartful, fun joke
That she would be here, surprise
But babe, welcome home!

Home-going

She lived life fully, enjoyably
Surrounded by family, jovially
But the cancer she fought
The damage that was wrought
Her strife was whole-hearted
Now she's pain-free, heavenly departed

Heart-homing

Do you ever think
Your heart has a homing beacon
Your heart is a homing pigeon
Your heart has another, better half?

Do you ever think
Your heart strives for what it isn't
Your heart wants what it doesn't have
Your heart needs just something...off?

Do you ever know
What exactly your heart needs
What exactly will calm the emotional storms
What exactly is required to be whole?

Do you ever try
Something uncomfortable but new
Something different just for the skipped beats
Something you've always wanted to, but why
not?

Do you know
Where your heart home is
Where you are most comfortable
Where the beat harmonizes with another

Do you know/care/try/think.....home, your heart.

Head up, Heart open

In brilliant shades of pink and sapphire
Heart reaching to the moon
Stretching along the horizon line
Yawning to the full-bloomed

Tufts of whiteness follow
Dancing across the mass
Spilling baby dew drops
As slowly and gracefully they pass

Light as far as the eye can see
Beautiful pinks and golds
Giving full effect of now
Of what this source does hold

Vows drift in the air
Promises of tomorrow and today
To give off energy and hope
Just keep your head up to be okay

The sky is almost lit now
No darkness seen by one
A new day bright and early
All ready by the sun

Heart Song

Staying up so late at night
You had a good day, why must you end it now
The lights went out 20 minutes ago
Your dog is snoring
But you think I mustn't sleep, I mustn't
Numbness, that sneaky feel, crawls up your legs
And bizz, they're gone, they can't move an inch
You have lost your legs, your way of
transport---now what
Your eyes must not close, they mustn't
Limpness ties your arms in knots
They fall out with a gentle sigh
You body is a natural follower, so it too goes the
way of your arms and legs
Your stomach waiting anxiously for the next
meal
It silences with a grumble
Dizziness over comes your head
And zap, it's gone dead, dead asleep that is
But you must not go to sleep, you mustn't
I mustn't sleep you think I mustn't close my
eyes
Go to bed…. Your next day's schedule flashes
before your eyes...
An echoing voice.... Go to bed

No, you resist the words, no
My eyes are the strongest, they've lasted the
longest
But time runs out for your weary little pupils
You get blurry vision
You rub your eyes irritably and sigh
Now the words are taking over, they repeat
throughout your head
You now know where the "Go to bed" is
originating
Your heart, your heart, its song increasing in
volume, ready for rest
Go to bed, Go to bed, Go to bed
Eyelids drooping, no light, goodnight

De Corazón

Salvaje de corazón
Joven y libre
Espera pacientemente
A todos los sueños

Feroz de corazón
Joven y desatado
Espera pacientemente
A todos los deseos

El corazón es
Feroz
Salvaje
....Tuyo

In my Heart

My mind a torrent
Stress ever mounting
You, my love, my heart
My only reprieve
To hold you close
To hear your voice
I am temporarily
Released from
My abyss

....Et mon coeur pour toujours

Et mon coeur pour toujours
Je t'aime ce monde
L'herbe, les arbres
Les oiseaux, les abeilles

Les chiens qui aboient
Les chats qui miaulent
Les vents qui chantent
Le ciel qui peint

Les belles montagnes
Les mers magnifiques
Les vastes plaines
Le plein air

Je t'aime mère terre
Ma dame, notre dame
Cette dame
Merci mademoiselle

Reste propre, reste la nôtre.

Young at Heart

Young and wild and free
The heart beats BA BUMP BA BUMP
Going going....gone

With all my Heart

If I could write a love poem
I guess it would be flowery and sweet
It would portray my feelings in writing
Of how being with you is such a treat

It would tell of how I love your smile
Your beautiful eyes and laugh too
It would tell why I found you to be perfect
Everything in it would be absolutely true

It would sing songs of inside jokes
Nights spent being up to no good
Deep intimate talks at 3 am in the morn
Intense feelings that were once misunderstood

It's hard to write a love poem
And say exactly what it is you feel
It would speak a language so precise
Words teeming with emotion and zeal

I guess I can't write a love poem
I guess that's too hard for me to do
To express everything with all my heart
I guess all I can say is – I love you

Have a Heart?

Heart
Red pumping
Muscular providing
Blood carrying
Nutrients, waste
Physical

Heart
Rhythmic beating
Four chambers
Valves controlling
The in and out
Technical

Heart
Eyes crying
Fast thumping
Chest aching
From the brokenness
Emotional

Heart
Deep feeling
Inner choosing
Strongly determining

What to do, how to react
Internal

Heart
Red pumping
Rhythmic beating
Fast thumping
Strongly determining
Have a...heart?

Happy at Heart

Hitting a ball with a baT
All the crowd waves the clotH
Pitch is fast and truE
POW the bunt is caught in the foul areA
YEAH the stands gleefully roaR
Another game for a team so greaT

<3

Life
Work, play
Being, learning, striving
Children, adults, ghosts, angels
Leaving, passing, expiring
End, gone
Death

The Queen of Hearts

What makes you
Queen of hearts?
Do you have the most hearts?
Have you broken the most hearts?
Can you draw hearts well?
Speak from the heart?
A hearty laugh?
Card tricks?
Or are you always the best bet?
Always there for others?
Always there for yourself?
Always beating to your own drum?
Always this queen...of all hearts?

No Place like....Home

I know I fear the worst
The worst keeps me from having fun
My phobias are like a blanket
Covering me, shielding my heart from the real
world
I want to cure the sick, help the poor
But my blanket is so thick, so warm and cozy
I don't want to let in the worst
I couldn't take it off if I said "please"
Sitting in my fantasies
With a half full cup of dreams
Underneath my blanket
I sit, waiting for my cover to drift away
Bravery is like a hand
Reaching out to grasp your blanket
Pulling it off for awhile
Just for awhile
I have been waiting for the hand to come
To make me cold again with courage
To fold my blanket and put it
On the upmost shelf of my closet
Until that day comes I will sit in
My chair of life
It is comfy, home
But not as my cover of fears

Last Beat

The heart beats
one last time with
one last effort as the
final word is typed
ending the collection.